Patti O'Neill

# Placing Architecture

Landscape + Art = Architecture

Published by the A. K. Ilen Company
Limerick, Ireland

© Patti O'Neill

Book layout and cover design: Copper Reed Studio
Book design and content: Patti O'Neill

ISBN: 978-0-9547915-3-7

Printed in the Republic of Ireland by FX Press Ltd., Ennis, Ireland.

This publication has received support from the Heritage Council
under the 2007 Publications Grant Scheme.

# Content

## Foreword

It is so seldom that we encounter the work of an architect that fully engages the idea of landscape that at first we hesitate before it, not knowing what to think. Architects, so we have been conditioned to believe, design buildings, objects that sit upon one landscape or another, with some sensitivity to it or not, but fundamentally separated from it. Architects, so we have been taught, are not responsible for landscapes, but only for the tectonic fragments they scatter across them. The landscapes themselves are the responsibility of planners, government agencies representing the public interest, or specialized designers – landscape architects – who design the ground surfaces building architects do not, usually constructing gardens, parks and other public spaces. It is a division of professional labor to which we have become accustomed, but which leaves us totally unprepared to appreciate, and critically evaluate, the work we encounter in this book.

For Patti O'Neill, architecture and the landscape are one. In her work, they cannot exist without each other. Indeed, we cannot find in her drawings and designs where one begins and the other leaves off. There are discreet spaces and elements, just as there are distinct and separate trees in a forest, but they intertwine and interact in ways that speak of a complex harmony of differences. Hers is a subtle interweaving of shapes, colors, textures, but also of presences, of different modes of existence. In her projects, the tactile and conceptual engage in an especially constructive play. It is a new way of seeing the human and the natural together, in the aspect of its not only generous but, at the same time, particular embrace. This is highly original work. We have not seen it before.

In her projects, we find an inspiring direction for the future. Avoiding jargon, she creates a vivid series of designs, texts, and images exploring the ways previously assumed opposites can be reconciled with intelligence and beauty. Her directness sends a message of its own. Experience. Think. Feel. And draw. Forget the given categories and divisions. Be independent, be free, yet be precise. And be deliberate. In the deliberateness of her work, its unqualified intentionality, I perceive a profoundly ethical stance.

The burden is on us, now that the book, and the work of many years it represents, is in our hands. We have to reconsider our usual ways of thinking about landscape, and about architecture, if we are to experience the fullness and, yes, the joy of her vision.

Lebbeus Woods
5 November 2007, New York

## Introduction

*Placing Architecture* is a method of tailoring architecture to the natural environment to create a sense of place and to inspire sustainable and nature-appreciating lifestyles.

From an early age I have been interested in how society could live more in unison with its natural surroundings. I often feel we distance and alienate ourselves from nature; we see it as something that needs to be controlled to attain physical and mental comfort. Yet I believe humans have a fundamental requirement for connectivity: a need to connect to people, nature and the world at large.

At college I was exposed to different methods of architecture, but most addressed the need to be protected from nature. The environment was only taken into account where structurally required from an engineering viewpoint. However, I felt these methods did little to secure a sense of connectivity with our surroundings. Thus, my quest for a personal philosophy of architecture had only just begun.

The colourful pages to follow in this book invite you on a six-year journey of exploration, investigation and study. Described is a method of architecture employing a strong artistically and intuitively-lead approach that brings the art in architecture to the foreground. It concludes with the placing of architecture in natural landscapes around the world. It is questionable if the results can still be classified as architecture as opposed to landscape installations or art works, yet they are spaces and enclosures. Their functions depart from the conventional path, and bring back into focus a depth to life which is often out of reach. The buildings in this book evoke meditations on Change, Time and the Cycle of Life and Death.

### A Biography: *The Exploration of Childhood Abodes*

At the start I chose three contrasting natural landscapes, as untouched as possible by human influence. The projects are *Dune Landscape by the Sea*, set on the North Sea Coast in Germany; *Desertscape*, located in the high deserts of New Mexico, U.S.A.; and *Boglands*, set in Ireland. The choices were guided by childhood abodes located near these landscapes. I felt this previous connection would enhance my experience. I examined the archaic and native features of each habitat and its ecology, incorporating orientation and climate, as well as some of the cultural and aesthetical backdrops of the country.

### A Method of Architecture: *Landscape + Art = Architecture*

This method entails a prolonged on-site study of the landscapes through photography and painting. Back in the studio, key paintings are transformed into 3-dimensional objects. The next step involves returning to the topography of the landscape, choosing a location and enlarging, expanding and reassembling the objects into architecture. This method ensures that the architecture will have a sense of place and connectivity to the site, and by employing painting and sculpture, the architecture is guaranteed a strong aesthetic quality.

An Environmental Project:
*Creating a Connection to Our Natural Surroundings*
The results of the projects shown in this book are interactive buildings that solely address the uniqueness of the environments they are placed in. Their function is to bring the visitor closer to these primal and archaic worlds and encourage a deeper experience and awareness on a physical, mental and spiritual level. At the same time, in the case of *The Bog-Bubble*, they draw attention to our threatened landscapes and highlight the impending danger they are in if left unprotected. Therefore in essence, the projects carry the crucial message of Environmental Awareness.

At present, working in the commercial world of architecture, I am incorporating the key points of my philosophy in urban settings with building projects ranging from a shopping centre, a retirement village to a social re-generation masterplan. I am placing architecture that responds to its topographical and natural environment, to inspire active, nature-appreciating lifestyles.

I believe whether planning a city, a house, a garden layout, or even a walk, that giving the natural environment utmost priority results in an enhanced quality of life and integration into the natural world.

In the following pages you will find the detailed description of the three Environmental Projects describing my Method of Architecture:

– *Dune Landscape by the Sea* establishes the working method and reveals the subtle changes in and on such an ephemeral costal environment

– *Desertscape* takes the method through to a fully detailed architectural construction and discovers the timelessness of the arid inland context

– *Boglands* applies the method to a definite building proposal that unearths the cycle of life and death in a hidden landscape of a very different nature.

Patti O'Neill
September 2007, Limerick

# Dune Landscape by the Sea

## Travel and Work Account

The project Dune Landscape by the Sea confirmed my working method of deriving architecture from a specific location. The method I developed is common to all three projects.

For the research of this project I spent the summer of 1996 on the island of Sylt on the north coast of Germany. The first few weeks I lived in a small holiday unit of a high-rise building in the main town Westerland. To continue my stay I had to change my accommodation. A garage conversion situated far from the hustle and bustle of tourist life met my economic requirements.

Dispersed all over the island are many signs forbidding this, that and the other. Their strict and intimidating effect struck me even as a child visiting the island. Another observation from those visits was the covering and uncovering of large constructions, such as a lighthouse and military coastal protection installations from World War II, as well as houses that would have been situated inland at the time of their construction. All this architecture was eventually carried into the sea by heavy winter storms. This is how year to year the island is transformed.

My research on the island was influenced on the one hand by the raw architecture of the town of Westerland, on the other hand by the substantially larger part of the island's natural coastal landscape. Unfortunately, to walk in parts of this landscape is even prohibited by law. It was precisely this

inaccessibility that strengthened my desire to be closer to nature on the island and defined the task of developing a building. The intention was to provide an alternative to the no trespassing signs, while at the same time encouraging people to respect the natural surroundings. This building should primarily enable access to nature and at the same time help preserve respect for it.

How could the theoretical analysis of the problem be translated into the beginnings of a practical solution?

Suddenly, I was confronted with the limitations of the traditional methods of architecture I had been taught. Through spending long periods of time in the natural landscape, I intuitively discovered that walking, photographing and painting the landscape offered the best means of absorbing and interpreting.

The *Photography* shows the different architecture of the island, the different types of no entry signs and their wording as well as the paths laid through the dunes. The paths seemed to act as the sole points of entry to nature. And last but not least, the photographs show the landscape itself: the sand dunes, the beach, the sea and the sky.

The first *Landscape Studies* evolved using acrylic on paper. In strongly reduced form they show the contours of different elements of the landscape: dunes, beach, sea and sky. At one stage the view is towards the horizon of the sea, at another from the top of a dune overlooking the meandering water of the sheltered side of the island, then it follows a semi-abstract perspective looking down onto the divide between sea and land. And finally in the same reduced manner the view is directed towards the architecture of Westerland.

And gradually the focus left the natural settings and habitats. The next series of paintings liberated and concentrated themselves on a language of reduced outlines. I added some colours to build up the contrast to the given Nordic tones. In the end the theme became the play between the curved and the straight line.

At the end of a two-month period on the island the following three paintings emerged successively. They are subject to diverse interpretation due to their high abstraction and reduced state. In order to stay free from my own evoked associations, I had to concentrate and focus solely on what was in front of me. In consequence the following description reflects this scrutiny, vital at the time for the project to proceed.

*Painting I* - A blue rectangle is located in the centre of a wheat-yellow surface. This surface runs out and is met by a wave-shaped, aubergine-coloured surface. A short strip escapes in the direction of the blue rectangle.

*Painting II* - Dark green stripes with alternating different beige-toned stripes cross the page. In the bottom part a red wave swims, cutting the stripes in its path.

*Painting III* - A dark blue and a light beige surface share the page. A straight line turning curvaceous separates them. Finally it is broken up by rectangles of differing red tones and sizes. Another red rectangle is situated entirely in the beige surface.

*Landscape Studies*

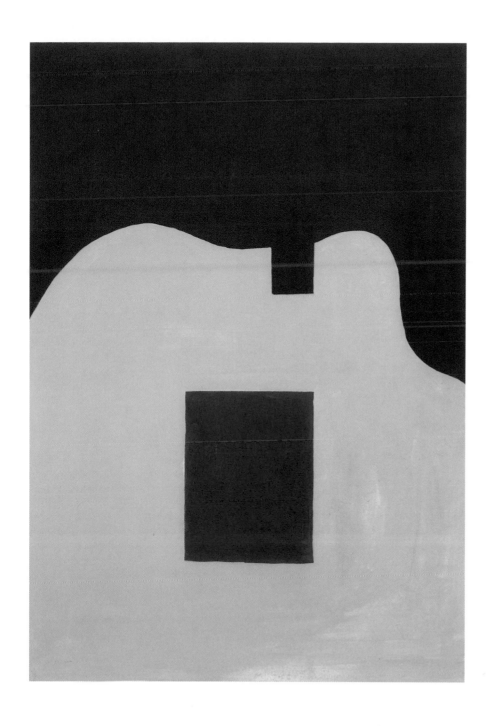

Painting I

Painting II

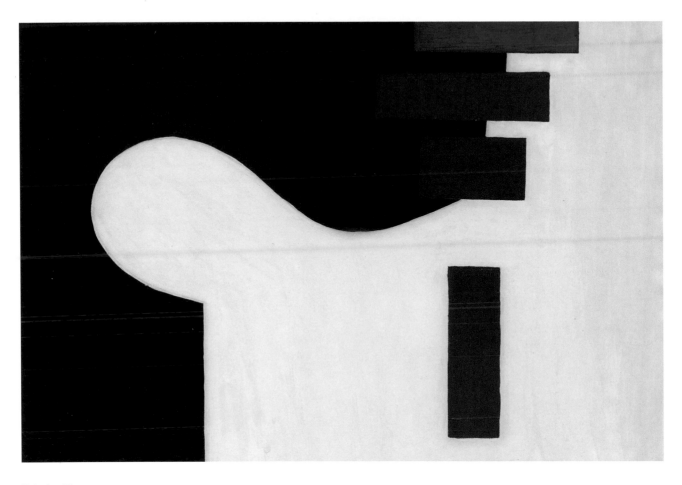

*Painting III*

At this stage I ended the research period and returned home. There I proceeded to paint with cleanly divided surfaces filled with flat colours. I imagined the coloured surfaces lying at different depths relative to each other and hence defining a space. A further painting with a blue rectangle hinted at a section through an object. With these paintings, including the ones done on location, I developed a sculptural repertoire.

Out of plywood, later painted over with acrylic, I built three objects all around the dimensions of 30 × 40 × 15cm. The views in plan were similar to *Paintings I-III* done on location.

*Object I* – An aubergine coloured volume rises in the shape of a wave and is cut off at right angles. This slice is marked by a yellow colour. A blue rectangular imprint sinks into the volume from the horizontal slice. A thin yellow wall pulls through the volume alongside the blue imprint.

*Object II* – A curving line in the vertical plane and a straight line in the horizontal plane cut through a red volume. These incisions are distinguished by a dark green colour. It reveals long, beige, rectangular imprints that tilt in different angles within the red volume. The vertical section shows the rectangular imprints being carved into and partially stretching through the red volume.

*Object III* - A light beige waved surface cuts and spills onto a dark blue volume. At one stage the horizontal section creates a light beige, at another, a dark blue vertical surface. At one point it is straight, at another it is curved. The vertical surface carries the imprint of three cubes of differing red tones and sizes. They sink into and partially cut through the blue volume. A further red imprint is placed in the centre of the beige surface passing right through the volume.

*Studies leading to Objects*

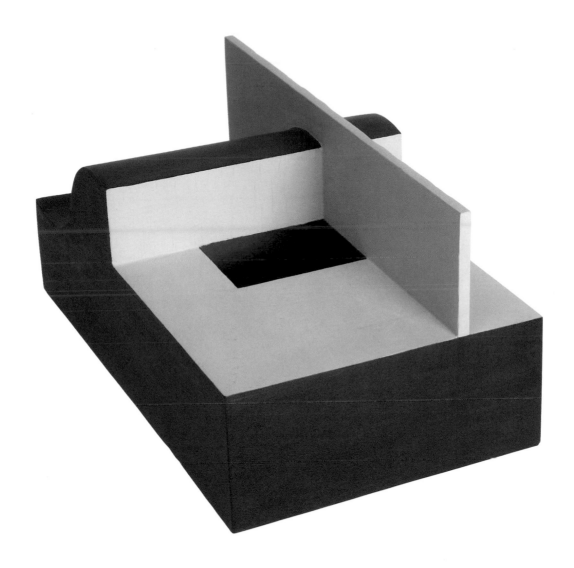

*Object I*

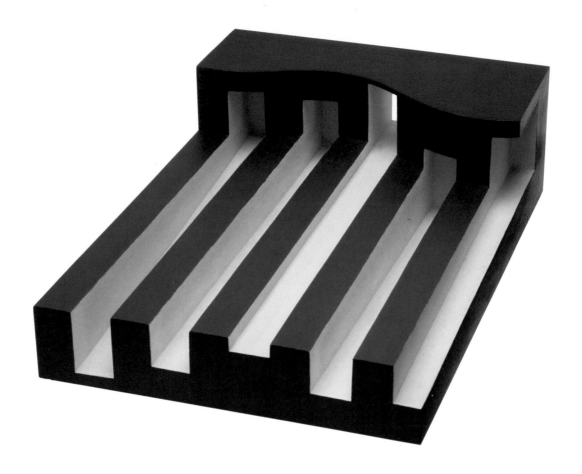

*Object II*

*Object III*

In search of a spatial interpretation of these objects I began by painting them seen from the inside, stretched and torn apart. This gave me experience and practice in inverting and dividing up the volumes as well as dispersing them into separate elements.

*Incision + Invertion + Dispersion*

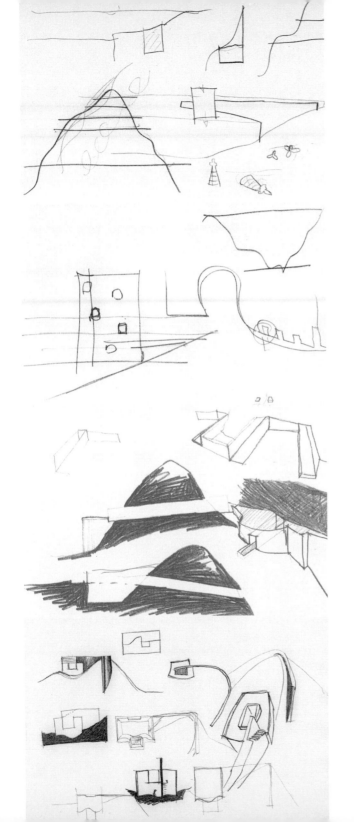

The next step brought me back into the landscape I had started out from. In it I searched for three specific sites suitable for the three objects. The result was the following selection:

For *Object I* because of the centred blue rectangle
 a freestanding conical shaped dune.
For *Object II* reminiscent of its distinct long beige rectangles
– a long extended dune continuing in the same angle.
For the *Object III* inspired by the colours blue and beige
– the site on the seacoast.

By means of sketches and model-making, an architecture developed in a close dialogue between the objects and their designated topographies. In a game like approach without strict rules, the surfaces, shapes and colours were extracted, inverted or even entirely removed from the objects.

*Sketching towards Architecture*

# Architecture

### The Beach

In the case of the object allocated to the seacoast, the waved light beige surface and the straight dark blue surface were replaced by the beach and the sea. At their intersection, the red cube imprints from the object were inverted into red cubes of solid volume.

### The Longitudinal Dune

The long beige rectangles translated into long incisions stretching through the longitudinal dune, as they did through the red volume of the object.

### The Conical Dune

The last object that was assigned to the conical dune was more complicated. It was a building with enclosed spaces. The aubergine volume developed into a space that continued to hold the blue rectangular imprint. As in the object, the imprint remained the same except that the blue surfaces became translucent and consequently visible from within the building. The yellow wall elongated and grew to a partially accessible corridor acting as a guide into and through the building.

The subject of meditation for Dune Landscape by the Sea, although not built can still be experienced through the graphical presentation, which continues on the same lines as the paintings and objects. With acrylic on heavy paper, lightly abstract, strongly reduced and flat colour surfaces characterize the architectural presentation.

## Changes in and on a Dune Landscape by the Sea

The movements within the landscape and the accompanying changes to the horizontal and vertical planes are made apparent with the help of two installations. In a third installation the focus is on a room, which through its design, directs the attention to the inner human landscape.

*Site plan*

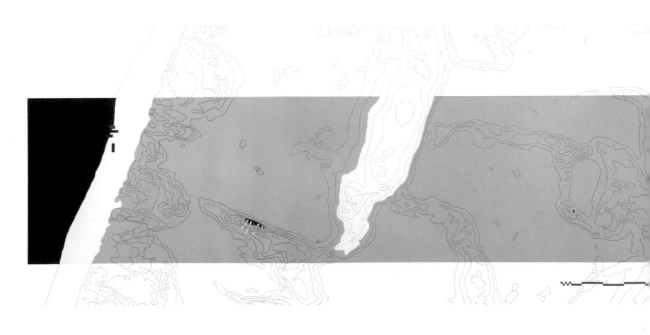

### Changes in the Horizontal Plane

Four concrete cubes stand on the coastline in the water. They are different sizes and are coloured in different red tones. They act as a tangible measure and indicator in the sea, revealing the spatial changes in the horizontal created by the tidal changes.

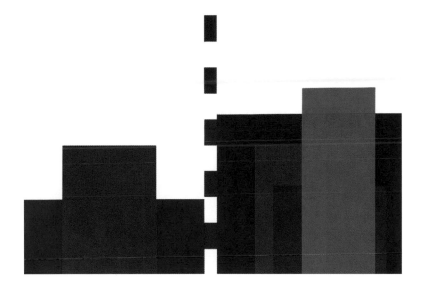

*The Beach*

## Changes in the Vertical Plane

Further inland, four accessible tunnels penetrate a wandering sand dune. Their entry is made possible by an adjustable platform. The movement of the sand dune causes the concrete tunnels to change their angles: as a result there is a shift of the landscape and sky in the picture, seen as if through a large telescope. In the light of these slow-changing pictures, the spatial changes in the vertical become visible.

*The Longitudinal Dune*

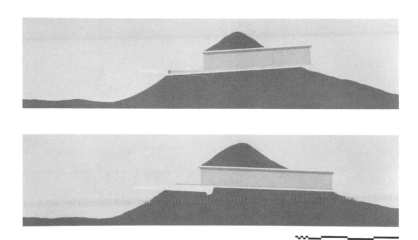

## Changes in the Inner Landscape

In the third installation a guiding wall leads to the highest point of a dune. The whole surrounding landscape can be taken in from here. The wall continues to guide into a building. Passing through a courtyard, where the walls and floor are of blue, opaque glass, one reaches steps leading down to a room. It is situated below the glazed courtyard which floods the space with diffused, blue light. Here there is neither farsightedness nor clarity. The visual effect is similar to being underwater.

The sharp transition, from the farsightedness at the top of the dune to the diffused and shapeless vision in the building's interior, facilitates the entry to one's inner world. With this room holding no clear boundaries, no distractions from the outside world, the inner landscape can spread itself out.

The experience of the two other installations in the natural landscape have stimulated the reflection on change. Through the Conical Dune building, where the inner world has entered the field of vision, the theme of change is transferred onto one's own life. Reflection and contemplation on events that have given rise to change becomes possible. Finally, against the backdrop of change, we see what remains constant in our lives.

*The Conical Dune*

# Desertscape

## Travel and Work Account

The project Desertscape not only stands in high contrast to the one before but also it takes a step further. My aim was to develop a concept to the point where it could theoretically be built. This meant tackling the technical and construction aspects of the architecture as well as the financial end.

During my early childhood in Los Angeles, we made trips all over the Southwest of the United States. With this knowledge, as well as the influence of Georgia O'Keeffe's biography, I decided to investigate the landscapes of New Mexico, USA.

This journey was a step more adventurous than the previous one, due to the distance from home and the size of the territory I was going to explore. A major anxiety was that I knew nobody in that area, and I was a woman travelling alone. While preparing for the journey, I got to know through a friend of a friend the Stuttgart Balloon Club. They were going to take part in the biggest Balloon Fiesta in the world that autumn of 1997 in Albuquerque, New Mexico. After a little balloon training, I joined them on their excursion to the USA.

During the ballooning fortnight I saw the vastness of the landscape from the air, but back on the ground the landscape seemed just as endless.

The local people revealed themselves to be extremely hospitable. It wasn't long until I received invitations from native Balloonists families to come stay in their homes in Albuquerque after the Fiesta was over. For further explorations of the state, I first had to buy a car.

My excursions entailed accompanying other ballooning events throughout New Mexico, joining an ecological volunteer group on a clean-up-a-hiking-trail camping weekend, visiting other people's family members and friends in far parts of the state and house-sitting a mobile home situated in the middle of the desert. The nearest I got to settling down was in the final month, when I borrowed a mobile home and based myself in a trailer park in Albuquerque.

Previous to my stay I had heard of the great heritage left from ancient Native American societies still existing in New Mexico. I was expecting a society somewhat in tune with and orientated towards nature. What I saw, however, was a society living spread out in the desert in homes with swimming pools, cars and malls. Even in winter every structure, every enclosure, every business and every home was air-conditioned and therefore completely cut off from nature.

For my research I used similar methods as in the first project, only I travelled by car. From within the car, the surroundings seemed removed and distant, as if looking at a film screen. I would have liked to hike through the landscape, but the distances were too great. Ultimately, I imagined travelling on horseback the ideal way to experience the desert. Instead, I sought sites off the beaten track and stationed the car. There I spent hours taking photos, painting and trying to let the surrounding desert soak in.

*Sunset over Tullarosa Basin*

I began by observing the light reflecting off the vast open planes of the land. I discovered that the light created differently coloured layers depending on the surface and the angle at which the land was tilted towards the sun. The watercolour painting, *Sunset over Tullarosa Basin*, describes the coloured layers on the horizontal plane.

*Layer I*

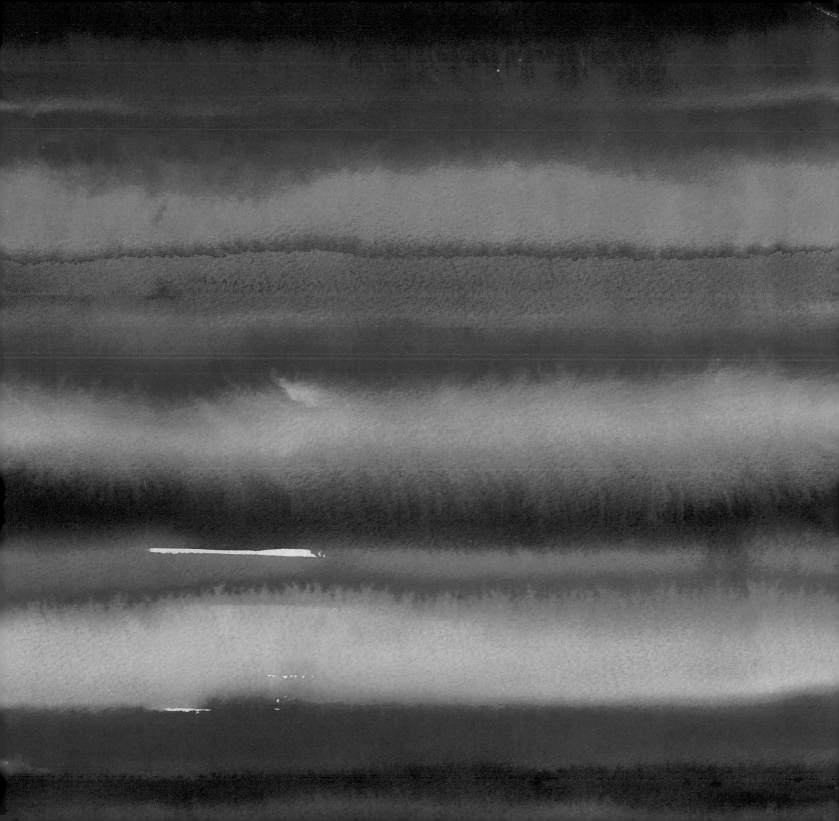

*Echo Amphitheatre in O'Keeffe Country*

Another theme I investigated was the sediment layers visible
in canyons and land faults. The series, *Echo Amphitheatre
in O'Keeffe Country*, shows these layers from the vertical plane
in the landscape.

In the evenings I continued searching for themes. I painted
layer upon layer of different shades of reds and earth tones.
This developed into the series: *Layers*. At first I saw no
connection to the landscape studies. If anything, they were
reminiscent of the woven carpets of the Native Americans.
In the end I found the connection in the final painting of
the series, *Echo Amphitheatre in O'Keeffe Country*. The
illustrated earth layers took on the characteristics of the
abstracted layers of the series *Layers*. With this I understood
that the series, *Layers*, unified them by creating an abstraction
of the horizontal and vertical landscape phenomena.

At this stage I had been in New Mexico for four months.
I now had enough material to go home. Also, my car had
just died on me on a journey through Death Valley!

*Layer II*

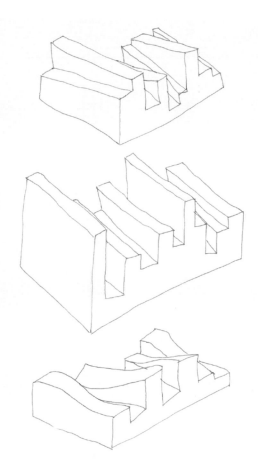

*Experiments leading to Drill Cores*

Focussing now solely on the transition between the layers,
I experimented with oil paint on canvas. The oil paint
basically only repeated the effect of the watercolours.
Finally, I took the oil canvases and mounted them
to long rectangular wooden boxes making them
reminiscent of *Drill Cores* used in earth layer sampling.

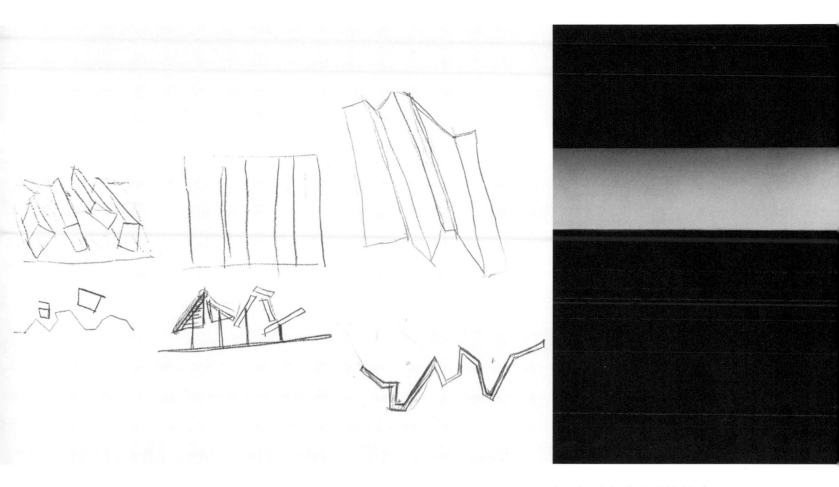

*Experiments leading to Folded Surface*

After trial and error and many dead-ends, I returned to the idea of observing the colour gradient on surfaces that are tilted at different angles to a light source. With rubber sheets that didn't reflect the light, I was able to recreate different colour gradients on tilted surfaces. This is illustrated in the object *Folded Surface*, in which large red and white rubber sheets are attached to plywood and joined together at different angles.

*Drill Cores*

*Folded Surface*

*Space Study I*

*Space Study II*

Continuing with the theme of light, I studied the transition between red and blue. I discovered that space and surfaces were required to perceive these colour gradients.

Taking the *Drill Cores* as the starting point, I used different red-coloured film to represent the layers. They are attached around a rectangular wooden frame. Within the frame, the layers are subdivided by translucent paper. With this object *Space Study I*, I studied the red shadows that were cast onto the ground as well as onto the internal translucent surfaces.

Based on *Folded Surface*, I built a new model using red film. The result was two overlaying folded surfaces suspended in a wooden framework painted grey. Observing and experimenting with light on *Space Study II* was interesting, but the multitude of folded surfaces produced very undefined projections.

Concentrating on this particular projection I returned to the *Folded Surface* with a slide projector. I mounted different red-coloured film strips on to a glass slide and projected them onto *Folded Surface*. The red layers from the slides, as well as those on the object, merged, making everything somewhat indistinguishable. Then I built a new folded surface of white cloth wrapped around several rods suspended in a white box. This time the projections of the red layer slides appeared with clearer transitions.

The next challenge was to transform these objects and studies into architecture. I had three elements: the rectangular volume with red-coloured film layers, the translucent folded surfaces, and light. With pencil and paper I proceeded.

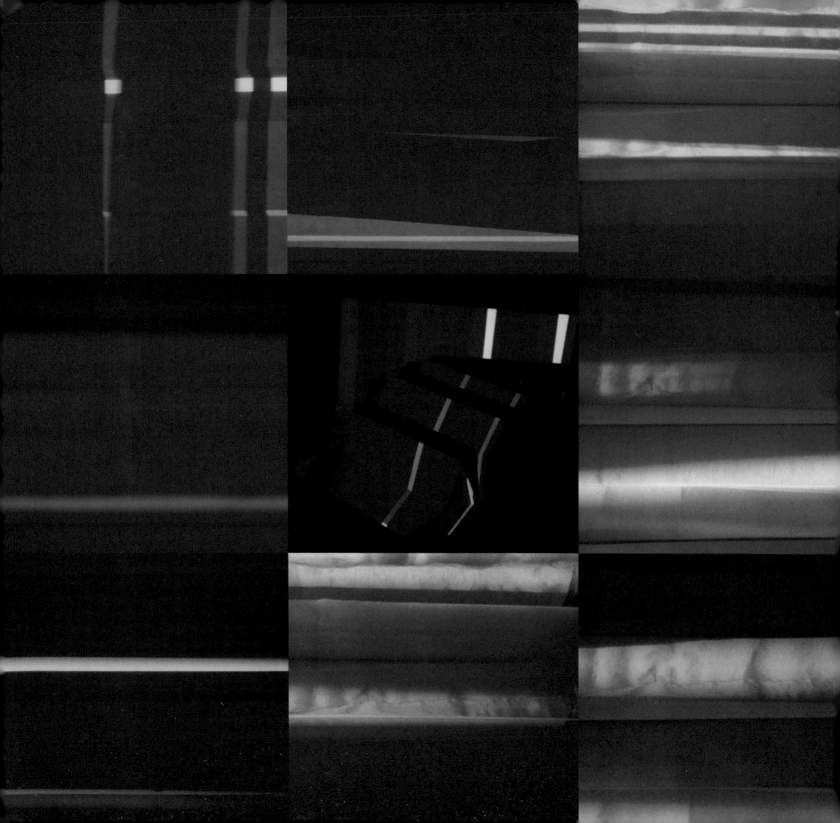

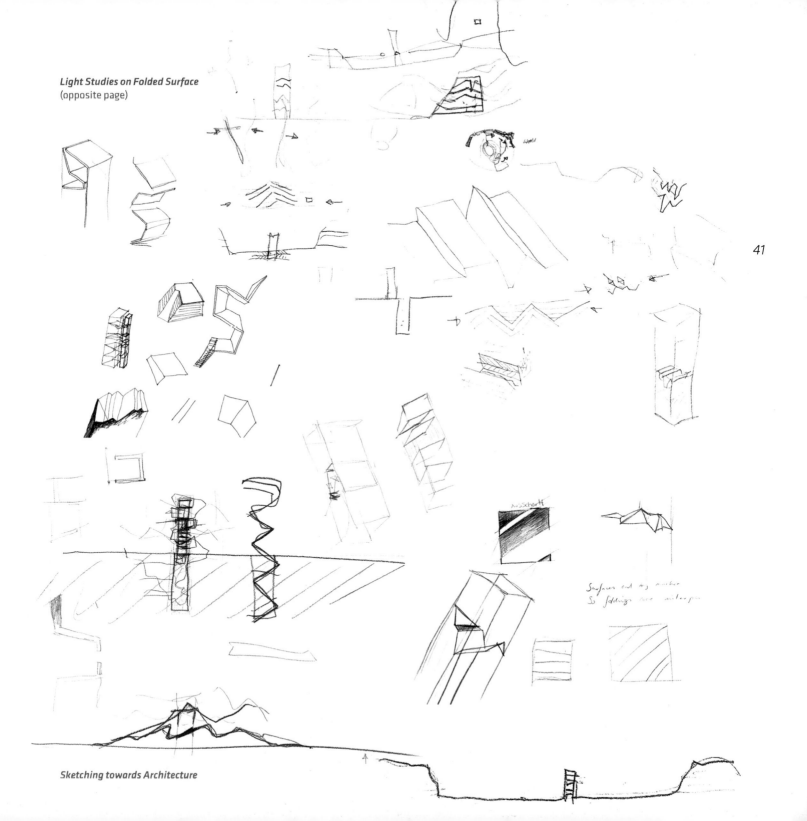

*Light Studies on Folded Surface*
(opposite page)

41

*Sketching towards Architecture*

# Architecture

### *The Tower*

The result is the tower: a long rectangle with different red-coloured film layers on the exterior and suspended in the interior and within each of the layers, translucent folded surfaces.

The tower is not a viewing platform in this endless landscape. Far more it is an introverted installation, one that can not be entered. Only by standing outside and looking into the tower can one observe the projections of the sun recording the passing of time onto the folded surfaces. A 20-minute video describes its course on the projection surfaces in the interior.

## Construction

With the aid of a model, I was able to give the tower its proportions. I dimensioned the projection surface in the interior to be seven by seven meters. (This is the dimension I discovered that was required to perceive the moving shadows created by the sun with the naked eye.) In consequence, the height of the tower reaches 35 meters. In an urban context this height is perceived as large, yet here it is dwarfed by the vastness of this desert landscape.

To avoid the construction casting additional shadows, the coloured glass itself becomes the load-bearing element. Through its own weight it holds itself down to the ground and is anchored by a concrete foundation. Tension cables running vertically through the four corners hold it together to withstand horizontal wind pressures. Smaller cables were set horizontally at 4.5 meter intervals, to tie the glass panels together. The construction was structurally designed and verified and a cost estimate calculated by Rob Nijsse of ABT Consulting Engineers in Holland.

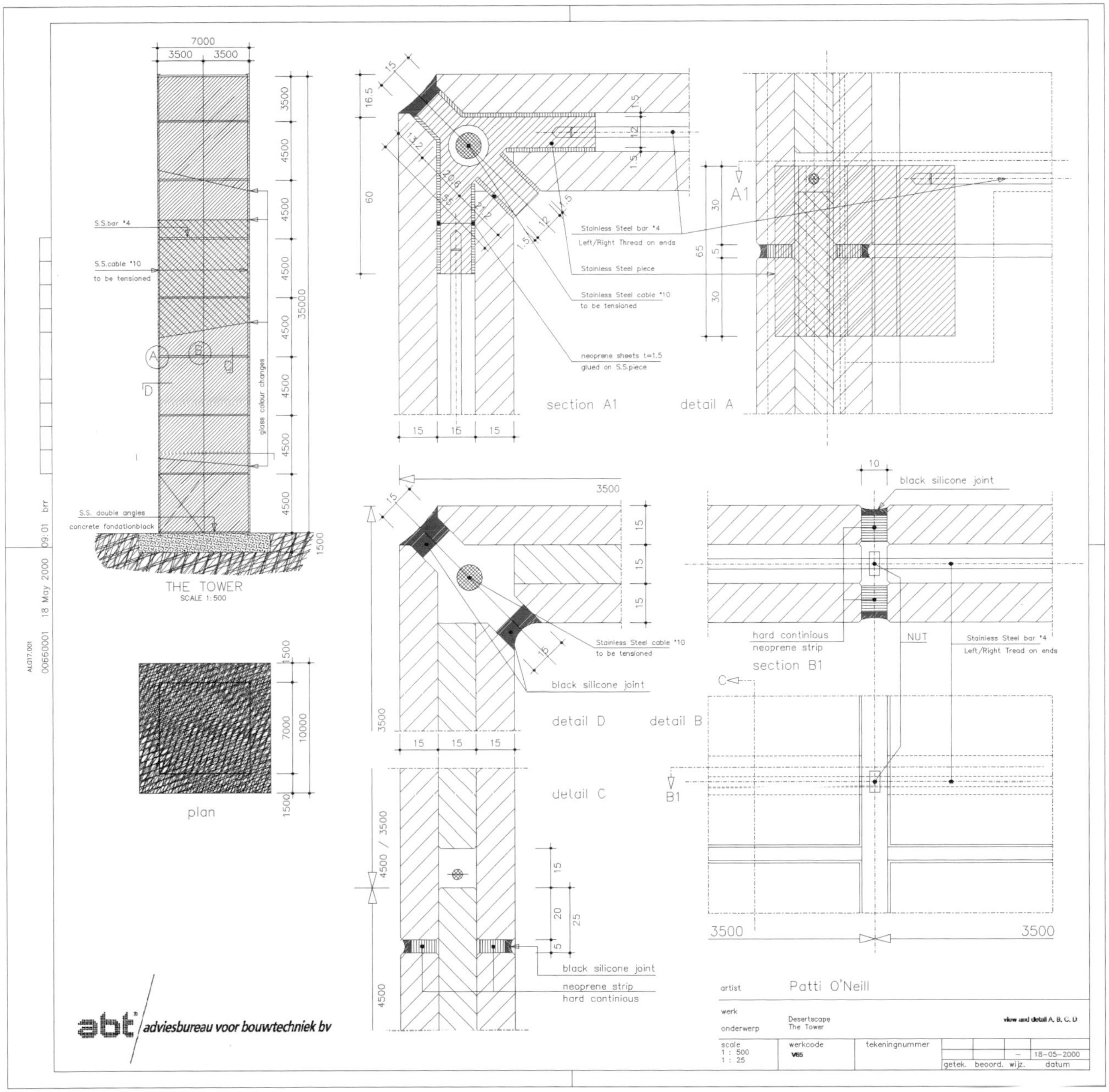

7000
3500
3500
S.S.bar *4
S.S.cable *10
to be tensioned
glass colour changes
35000
S.S. double angles
concrete fondationblock
THE TOWER
SCALE 1:500
plan
7000
10000
1500
00660001 18 May 2000 09:01 brr
ALG17.001
Stainless Steel bar *4
Left/Right Thread on ends
Stainless Steel piece
Stainless Steel cable *10
to be tensioned
neoprene sheets t=1.5
glued on S.S.piece
section A1
detail A
A1
black silicone joint
hard continious
neoprene strip
section B1
NUT
Stainless Steel bar *4
Left/Right Tread on ends
detail D
detail B
detail C
B1
black silicone joint
neoprene strip
hard continious
3500
abt adviesbureau voor bouwtechniek bv
artist
Patti O'Neill
werk
onderwerp
Desertscape
The Tower
view and detail A, B, C, D
scale
1 : 500
1 : 25
werkcode
tekeningnummer
18-05-2000
getek. beoord. wijz. datum


Engineer's Drawing

### Reds

*Part 1: Earth Time*
Macro shots: **Layers**
Different shades of red, beige, purple pass slowly from
the bottom to the top of the screen – a stroll through
the layers of the earth created over millions of years.

*Part 2: Day Time*
Macro shots: **The Tower**
Ten time-lapse sequences, in which the sunlight falls
through the coloured glass onto the folded surfaces in the
interior of the tower model. The moving colours document
the course of the sun through the passing of one day.

*Reds (video stills)*

### The Experience of the Time Dimension

There are few points of reference in the vast and empty desert of New Mexico. The passing of Time is one of them. It becomes visible during daytime through the course of the sun. Larger dimensions of time are documented in the different coloured sediment layers visible in the steep coastlines of the vanished prehistoric ocean. The layers offer a visual image of the time required for their creation. These two different time-scales are addressed in the architecture of the tower. It is made up of different red-coloured glass panes which depict the large time-spans in the earth's history. Suspended in between these layers are wafer-thin, translucent, folded surfaces that represent, as it were, an excerpt of a day within that layer.

So with this installation the large time-spans are put in relationship to the more foreseeable duration of a day. Depending on the position of the sun shining through the glass layers, the patterns of the shadows projected onto of the folded surfaces within change slowly but steadily.

They inspire meditation on the passing of a single day amidst a surrounding that displays the passing of substantially greater time-spaces. This in turn places our own lifetime in perspective with the earth's time.

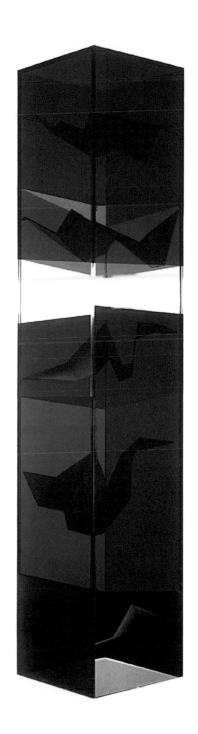

*The Tower*

# Boglands

## Travel and Work Account

The final part in the series *Placing Architecture* is in Ireland, the country where I spent my childhood school years. While travelling the country searching for a landscape, I decided this project would result in a definite building proposal. With the first project I had strengthened my working method, with the second, I had secured my ability to solve the technical construction issues. With this experience I now felt confident enough to be able to steer the design, keeping it to a feasible scale yet still expressing my concerns.

In the summer of 1998 I began my research. At first it was unclear what part of Ireland or what type of landscape I was searching for. My first longer excursion was on the West Coast, to Inish Mór of the Aran Islands where I was based for 3 months. Other trips included sojourns in Connemarra, north Co. Mayo, Co. Clare, Co. Tipperary, Co. Monaghan and Northern Ireland. For most of the time I stayed in youth hostels as well as artist centres.

The common denominator of my extensive travels was the Boglands. Photographs show different bog landscapes at different times of the year. Details reveal the saturation of the bog as well as its rich and diverse vegetation. Other images describe how areas in the midst of endless bog landscapes have been drained to create green pastures for livestock. And finally a series of photos document barren infertile landscapes, previously striped for turf.

The sites for painting also varied strongly from a grass field, to the rocky Atlantic coast, to a peat land bog. *Paintings I – III* describe the settings in an abstract manner, resulting in an abundance of organic shapes softly moving and circling around each other. The flowing, compactly intertwining shapes hold a tight boundary yet respond to each other by taking on the neighbouring forms. The colours are unrestricted, strong, bright and plentiful.

In the next step, wanting to transform paintings into objects, the paintings appeared too complicated and overflowing with shapes. I couldn't find any method in the entanglement and their complexity. So I began isolating details out of the paintings done on location. I was seeking to simplify the shapes and the movement in the compositions. What eventually evolved were bubble-like structures suspended in a plasmic mass. But at this stage I was at a complete loss as how to translate something which appeared so fluid, into a fixed three-dimensional shape. I had worked myself into a cul-de-sac.

50

*Detail Paintings*
(opposite page)

*Paper Cuttings*

Two years later I gave it another try. I took the *Detail Painting* with the two red-cupped shapes suspended in a pink mass as a starting point. This appeared to be the most reduced and simplified of all the previous studies. Sieving away the pink mass, I concentrated on the red shapes.

I painted two intertwining, differently coloured red shapes with acrylic on thick paper. The left over white space was cut away. Then I developed the series *Paper Cuttings* with the two shapes appearing in different juxtapositions. Through the series I hoped to evoke movement. However, I came to the conclusion that the intertwining organic shapes expressed movement in themselves without the help of a series.

To create a volume I took the simplest, most reduced stage of the series and attached it onto a 20 mm wood panel. *Relief I* suggests and enhances the sought after bubble effect.

In the reliefs that followed I used three colours and shapes. *Relief II* shows a blue pebble-like shape, behind which a green ribbon wraps around a beige bubble shape.

*Relief I*

*Relief II*

The next stage involved increasing the plasticity of the reliefs. Concentrating on the theme of embracing shapes, I continued with pencil and paper. *Drawings I–III* illustrate some of the many possible combinations and constellations.

Returning to my accustomed working method, I began looking for a specific location. On another journey through Ireland I still seemed unable to decide on a site. Although having explored half the country, there seemed to be no particular area that stood out from the others.

*Drawing I–III*

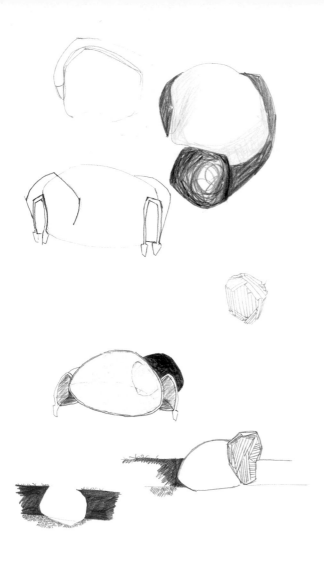

One day on the West Coast in a B & B overlooking a Bog landscape, I developed a series of sketches interpreting *Relief II* as a spatial structure in the landscape. *Sketching towards Architecture* describes the alterations. The green ribbon, wrapping itself around the beige bubble, transforms into a corridor. The blue pebble-like shape becomes an opening enabling access. And as the beige bubble submerges into the ground, the green encasing corridor releases its grip and lies in the surrounding peat acting as the entry tunnel.

It wasn't until then I realised that the bubble didn't have to have a specific location; it just needed to be placed in an appropriate Bogland.

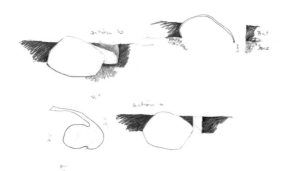

*Sketching towards Architecture*

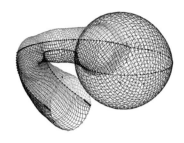

# Architecture

### The Bog-Bubble

This project creates an awareness of the uniqueness of the Boglands and the impending danger they are in. A peat layer tells the story of up to twelve thousand years of climatic changes and happenings. The damage to these landscapes through large-scale excavation and land drainage is irreversible. The installation of the Bog-Bubble structure is to draw attention to the cause of the Boglands and the need for their protection.

The Bog-Bubble is an accessible, translucent, double-membrane pneumatic structure. A round bubble-like shape reaches an approximate interior 4 meter height, a 4 meter width and a 6 meter length. It is submerged two-thirds into the Bog. The opening of the Bubble lies under the earth's surface. Lying in an excavated trench is another pneumatic tunnel structure enabling access to the Bubble.

Bogs are wet and marshy and difficult to walk on. The Bog-Bubble will be placed as close as possible to the Bog boundary. Large discarded wooden railway sleepers will bridge the remaining distance to the nearest solid ground.

It is envisioned that the Bog-Bubble be placed in centres that already attract visitors offering information and insight to the Bogs. The inclusion of this architectural feature will permit an additional experience of the Bog. It is also imaginable that the installation could wander through different Boglands, staying for the duration of one or two years at each location.

The *Computer Images I–II* show sections of the Bog-Bubble and its access tunnel superimposed in an abstract Bog landscape.

### Construction

The application of *Pneumatic Technology* comes from the desire to have as close a contact as possible to the Boglands. If you dig a hole in the Boglands, the hole immediately fills with water, making it inaccessible. A pneumatic structure inflated in this hole will literally press the water away, providing a space for viewing the entire depth of the bog. This building technique is also environmentally friendly, easy to erect and to remove. It neither employs large quantities of building material nor leaves them behind as waste. In addition, pneumatic structures present the possibility of creating new fluid forms that differ from conventional geometry.

The unusual challenge here stems from the great demands on the light construction and material because of the high water table in the Bogs. The engineer Rosemarie Wagner calculated and evaluated a more favourable double-lined membrane construction, eliminating over-pressure within the Bubble. This guarantees a simple means of access, in other words, no air lock is needed. The construction will be anchored by sand filled into the expanded double-lined membrane cavity at the bottom of the Bog-Bubble. The Technical University of Berlin employed modern, non-linear methods of calculation for the membrane construction. Coated, protected textiles will be used for the membrane, textiles that fulfil the optical requirements of transparency and the dispersion of light

*Engineer's Model*
(above)
**The Bog-Bubble**
*Computer Image I*

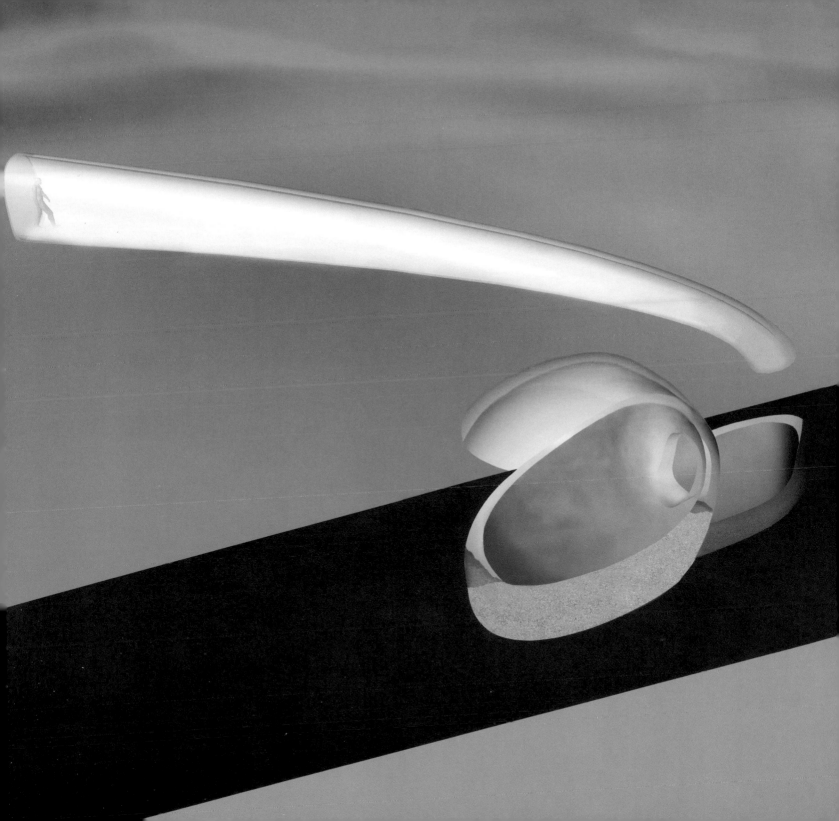

**The Cycle of 'Life and Death' in the Bogs**

Peat is the product of partially decomposed dead plant and animal matter in an airtight surrounding. This decay, to which every life form is subjected, has come to a stand still. The Boglands document a moment in this process: the cycle of life and death has stopped and is conserved.

Submerged in this landscape is the Bog-Bubble. With its round shape, it refers to the 'Cycle of Life', trapped in a state of suspension. In an ideal situation this feeling is transferred over to the visitor. It is uncertain if this is a womb or tomb. It offers a space of reflection and an outlook in both directions: the future as well as the past. The comprehension of the complete cycle of life and death and our own affiliation to it has the potential to relay strong feelings of security and warmth.

*The Bog-Bubble*
*Computer Image II*

## Conclusion

At the beginning of each project, all was unknown. I went open-minded to each location and allowed enough time to discover each landscape before putting pen to paper. Then, facilitated by the omission of a commercial brief, I was able to gain concentrated and profound experience in the fundamentals of Architecture: Shape, space, colour, light and material. The differences in the landscapes filtered through the work processes, as each of the projects engaged each landscape differently.

Dune Landscape by the Sea primarily concerns itself with *shape and colour.* The reason, I discovered, lies in the multiple shapes created by the sand and the sea. Desertscape focuses on *light and colour.* Only a full understanding and observation of the effects of light in the desert could have produced the construction, reflecting even in its detail the arid landscapes of New Mexico. The unusual aspect of working on the Boglands was that although I started out in full flight with strong colours, the emphasis shifted to *transparency and space.* These extremes can be compared to the transformation the Boglands undergo from a living surface to a dark compressed layer of peat.

The results - the Beach, the Longitudinal Dune, the Conical Dune, the Tower and the Bog-Bubble - are autonomous pieces of Architecture. They stand in the landscapes, bridging the scale between humans and the natural environment. They are ambassadors of Nature.

This book brings Nature to the centre of attention. To resolve the threat to humankind, we need to readdress our outlook and thinking. The way we live and the materials we use need to be revised. Most of the new materials have been developed for speedy construction and are no longer natural. They do not age gracefully, they develop no colourful patina, they do not breath and they do not readily decompose. We need to be realistic and think of tomorrow. We need our buildings to be equipped with renewable energy sources and non-toxic, recyclable materials. We need to find a way of modern living that addresses the before and after: a life-style that is replenishing.

Nature shows us how it is done. It shows us the cyclical way of survival. It shows us how balance is regained when imbalance occurs. This is why I believe Nature needs to be fundamentally and intrinsically interwoven in our thought processes as we design. The methodology described in this book can be applied to the many fields that are involved in creating our environments, including the daily one of how we lead our lives.

## Biography

**Patti O'Neill** is an Architect. Born in 1969, she grew up in the USA, Germany and Ireland. Between 1989–95 she studied architecture at the Academy of Fine Arts, Stuttgart, Germany. In 1993 under the guidance of the architect Lebbeus Woods in NYC, USA, she completed a project setting the direction for her future work.

After graduating she received grants and funding to pursue her own philosophy of architecture. These included:
1996-98 post-graduate grant from the state Baden-Württemberg / 1997 DAAD German oversees stipend / 1998 artist in residence in The Tyrone Gutherie Centre, Ireland / 1999 Visual Arts Bursary from The Irish Arts Council / 1999–2000 stipend at The Academy Schloss Solitude, Stuttgart / 2001 artist in residence in The Heinrich Böll Cottage, Achill Island, Ireland / 2002 stipend in The Art House Lukas, Ahrenshoop, from the Kulturfonds, Berlin. In 2004 she compiled the results of her research in this book.

Other activities have involved group exhibitions in The Municipal Gallery Backnang, Germany in 1997 *Motiv: Architektur;* publication in the magazine of BDA Der Architekt, Oct 1997, '*How can architecture be art?*'; and workshops in the School of Arts Berlin-Weißensee between 2001-3.

Since 2005 O'Neill has been working in Limerick, Ireland with a design-led architectural practice placing architecture.

*Dunelandscape by the Sea*
Photography of Objects and Plans: Copper Reed Studio
Support: Volker Albus

*Desertscape*
Photography of Objects: Michael Spaich
Reds (video) camera, cut: Susanne Schüle, Deirdre Green
Engineering: Rob Nijsse

*Boglands*
Photography of Reliefs: Copper Reed Studio
Computer Image I-II: Karin Sturm
Engineering: Rosmarie Wagner and TU-Berlin

Editing: Martha Hughes, Ulrich Schlotmann, Stefan Wiessner

The projects received support from:
Landesförderung Baden-Württemberg
DAAD Deutscher Akademischer Austausch Dienst
The Irish Arts Council
The Tyrone Guthrie Centre
Akademie Schloss Solitude
Achill Heinrich Böll Committee
Stiftung Kulturfonds Berlin

Thanks for the support and encouragement throughout the years to
Barbara Stelzer-O'Neill, Don O'Neill, Hedwig Stelzer, Gudrun
Binder, Giuliana Corsini, Caroline Stelzer and Annelene Meyer.

A special thanks to the A.K. Ilen Company for the publication.

This publication received support from:

Limerick City Council

Limerick County Council

*Comhairle Contae Thiobraid Árann Thuaidh*
**North Tipperary County Council**